THE

MANOPAUSE

MANUAL

How to make the most of your midlife crisis

By

PK Munroe

Contents

Introduction

People have been making jokes about the 'male menopause' for a very long time – too long, in fact. What is so funny about balding men buying sports cars, taking up hobbies, or re-forming our boyhood rock bands? Why shouldn't we?

Here at last the condition is treated with the sympathy and seriousness it deserves. Instead of mockery, I offer useful guidance so that any man can enjoy his manopause, rather than feeling depressed, guilty or furtive.

Women, especially the ones we are married to, tend to poke fun at manopausal impulses, or become worried by them (or both). This book provides vital advice about how to get your wife onside as you pursue a new hobby, or consider chucking in your job to take up the profitable and pleasurable business of goat-keeping.

Insight and advice is offered on the crucial male issues of growing a beard, avoiding exercise, becoming grumpy, seeking a philosophy, and acquiring and fitting out your shed. And the key question 'Do I need a sports car?' is examined in detail.

Often misleadingly called the 'male mid-life crisis', the manopause is just what it sounds like – a pause in a man's life, where we can look around for ideas that will add meaning, perhaps make us feel younger, but above all will be fun.

What is the manopause?

Sometime between the ages of 45 to 55, a man will start to experience some of these symptoms:

- Regularly wishing you could be somewhere else, without being sure where.

- Watching a dangerous sport on TV and thinking 'That doesn't look too difficult'.

- Wondering why your teenage rock band never made it big.

- Feeling envious of people on TV who appear to be your age, but are catching giant marlin off Zanzibar, pot-holing in the Lake District, or playing an electric guitar on stage.

- Lingering over sports cars in the street, checking out the bodywork and dashboard, and maybe even taking a photo.

- Ditto for large, powerful motorbikes.

- Admiring women in an art-gallery-admiring-the-pictures-and-sculpture way, rather than the usual way. They look good, but somehow you don't want them as badly as you want a sports car/motorbike/marlin-fishing trip to Zanzibar.

- Fantasising about a late career change or an early retirement

- Asking yourself why work has to consume so much of your time.

- Wondering 'is this all there is?' in moments when you're not distracted by work, sports cars, etc.

- Metaphorically hearing the sounds of doors closing all around you...

This is a serious list and there is a lot going on here. But if you are wondering, musing and daydreaming more than you ever have in the past 30 years, welcome to the first stage of the manopause.

What is the manopause? Put simply, it's a time when men pause. I mean really pause, not just take a breather. We stop, think, and wonder deeply about life. The fact that we do this while we are looking at a sports car, an attractive woman, or an array of electric guitars in a shop window, is not the point. Trust me, we are thinking deep thoughts.

As men know, the key to a happy life is to do what you want, as often as possible. But when we get to 50 and the manopause hits, we get the disturbing feeling that there must be something more to life. Part of us is still 18 (unfortunately not that part), but the rest of us feels suddenly, noticeably, different.

The symptoms of the manopause have a strange similarity to another thoughtful time of life – one's teenage years. Of course teenagers are famous for being thoughtless, but really this means not thinking about others – as teenagers we were very thoughtful indeed about ourselves.

Then the middle years take over, and we have to think about other things – wives, children, boss, job, football (possibly in that order).

So when the manopause strikes, it feels a lot like being a teenager again, wondering what life is all about, and what it would feel like to buy that guitar/sports car/shed.

But by now, you have acquired some advantages. You may have less hair, more waist and chins, and all those other unfair and allegedly humorous aspects of being in your fifties, but you are not entirely naive – you have some cunning, and with luck a little spare money. And you have some idea, perhaps gained from years of marriage watching a master, about how to get what you want without appearing unreasonable or selfish.

This is the real joy of the manopause: you can take advantage of it to find and fund something enjoyable that you actually want to do (rather than what you have been obliged to do all these years), and you know how to achieve it, while not looking too much like a monster of self-indulgence.

It's like being a teenager with control. Think about that!

Displacement behaviour?

Men in their late forties and fifties, it has been noticed, can often get fixated on an activity, a set of beliefs, a hobby, exercise, or indeed just about anything that's going.

The prevailing theory is that when men 'of a certain age' start behaving like this, it's all about sex.

How hobbies get started

The implication of this theory is that male behaviour at this age, whether it is train-spotting, gardening, cycling, recycling, metal-detecting, crossword-solving, or collecting military vehicles, can all be traced back to procreation, or rather the lack of it. A man who is past the normal age for having children, so we are told, is looking for 'displacement activities' to fill the vast psychological hole that has now appeared. So instead of making babies, we start milking goats or hunting for buried treasure.

The idea is sheer nonsense, of course. Even as boys we had spare-time hobbies – in fact especially as boys, when one's days were filled with fun and interesting hobby activities, because we had plenty of spare time.

Once we reached the age of dating, and our hormones kicked in, suddenly there was no time for boyhood fun. And then as husbands (and parents) we had no spare time at all.

It is only in later middle-age that men can begin, if we are strategic about it, to claw back a bit of the time we have longed for all these years. At last those fun hobbies and childhood activities start to beckon again.

If you want to be theoretical about it, you could argue that the procreative years were just an interruption in what should otherwise be a lifetime of hobbies. But I leave it to your judgement about the wisdom of using this argument, especially to one's wife and children.

And never let the words 'male obsessive behaviour' pass your ears without a challenge. It is simply mud-slinging. One person's obsession is another's enjoyable hobby.

When your roving eye turns to hobbies

It's a clear symptom of the manopause when the thought of a new hobby gets your pulse racing rather faster than the thought of an affair. The intentions are similar – to have a new adventure – but now you are dreaming of nothing more dangerous or challenging than throwing a dart, standing in a river holding a fishing rod, or milking a goat.

Finding a new hobby can be a bit like reverting to your teenage years. Symptoms include:

- Spending time in newsagents looking furtively at magazines, this time on the lower shelves

- Purchasing special interest books and magazines and hiding them at home. Yachting Monthly, Golf Digest, Trout and Salmon, Goats and Goatkeeping, and Metal Detective are just a few of the dozens of fascinating titles designed to appeal to men of a certain age

- Seeking confidential advice from your male friends who already have a thriving hobby.

- Sitting up late to watch TV programmes or visit websites that feature your new interest.

If you find yourself doing any of these things, it's clear that you need a new hobby. And why not? Taking up a hobby is one of the supreme pleasures of the manopause. And if you pick the wrong one, you can just bury the equipment in a cupboard, or put it up for sale on the internet, and choose again. No mess, no fuss.

What is a hobby?

First, it is something you wouldn't normally do with your wife or children, and something they are not tempted to join you in doing. Otherwise it's not a hobby in the true meaning of the word, which derives from the Greek for 'escape'[1]. So that rules out things like tennis, horse-riding, antiques-collecting or cookery, unless of course you are sure that your family are sufficiently bored by them to stay away.

Second, the best hobbies will put you together with like-minded male friends. If possible this should include friends from your youth – since the manopause points us back to our teenage years, who better to hang out with than our teenage mates? So this makes hobbies like train-spotting, stamp-collecting or astronomy feel second-best, unless you can find companions to join you.

---

[1] If it doesn't, it should do.

Third, a hobby is not undertaken for the benefit of the household. It may have a spin-off benefit (the vegetables one gets from gardening, or the trout from fishing), and if your hobby can somehow appear to be helping the household, so much the better. But this rules out DIY, home electrics, and car maintenance, for example – unless it's your own classic sports car, of course, which nobody else is allowed to go near.

It's not educational. 'Learning a language' is not really a hobby, although it may get you out of the house. Of course a hobby may involve some small amount of study, but it shouldn't be like going back to school.

Nor should a hobby be too much like work. You can't really call architecture or lorry-driving a hobby. The point is to get well away from work-day routines and responsibilities, yours or anyone else's.

So the main purpose of a hobby is to enjoy yourself, preferably with friends, while escaping from work and family. But of course you must never explain it like that.

Justifying your hobby

A hobby is not a selfish escape from your duties – certainly not. But to outsiders (this includes your family) it may unfortunately look that way. So before you get on with your new hobby, you have some lines to learn:

- **It's a new skill.** This can make the most obscure and idiotic hobby – classifying mountain lichens, for example – sound like the beginning of a new career.

- **It's something different.** Spoken with sufficient confidence, this gives the impression that you are an interesting fellow, the kind of self-motivated person who wishes to avoid becoming bored or stuck in a rut.

- **It keeps me busy.** The subtle implication is that otherwise you might be tempted by affairs, drink, or drugs. (If this doesn't work, try 'It keeps me out of mischief', or if you are poetically inclined, 'It fills the gaping void'.)

- **It keeps me fit.** An excellent button to push, since everyone is health-obsessed these days. And just about any hobby involves some kind of physical exercise.

- **It's better than watching TV.** A bit desperate, this one. After all, literally anything is better than watching most TV, even classifying lichens. Be careful not to use it if your chosen hobby involves screen time, for example important work like scrutinising, classifying and blogging about Carry On films.

- **I need it for my physical, mental, and spiritual wellbeing.** This is the nuclear option, the Big Bertha of justification, so use it sparingly. If pressed for an explanation, just hold your head and sigh, implying that they *just don't get it*.

You may feel that there is no need for you to believe any of these justifications – that they are a cynical way to get your family off your back. But in fact, to enjoy your hobby properly, it is better to believe them yourself.

If you are the strong and masterful type of husband who simply does whatever he wants without regard for his family, you are reading the wrong book. But frankly I doubt whether such men exist (or if they do, that they stay married very long). However if I'm wrong I'd be grateful if you could start a blog or something, to tell the rest of us about your methods. Thanks!

Finding the right hobby for you

It's all about what appeals to your personality type. Contrary to what the psychologists tell you, aside from the basics of avoiding pain and seeking pleasure, there are just a few very simple triggers in the male personality:

Individual competition. The dominant or 'Type A' male personality will compete with his fellows at just about anything. Those who want to compete, but can't, will gamble on just about anything instead. Those who compete and gamble to extremes tend to find themselves in jail, or the City.

Peace and quiet. 'I want to be alone' is attributed to the actress Greta Garbo, but the script was undoubtedly written by a man. To be left in peace for a few hours is a very common male fantasy.

Gadgets. It's a cliché because it's true. Even powerful, intellectual or artistic men are fascinated by gadgetry. High or low tech, we want to admire it, play with it, look inside and take it apart to figure out how it works. A hobby with constantly improving technology (ie. frequently updated or new gadgets) is ideal, since we can regularly buy ourselves a 'little treat'.

Nerdy. A vulgar shorthand for 'achieving mastery through the scientific method'. A fascination, bordering on obsession, with collecting, classifying, arranging and listing things, the obscurer the better.

Hunter-gathering. The urge is always there, even if it's masked by our modern lifestyles. Give a man a spade and watch these instincts re-emerge (he'll need a patch of ground too, of course). You may have noticed that men enjoy going to supermarkets without their partners. Shopping is a modern form of hunter-gathering, and it's well known that women never went on the hunt.

Team competition. Belonging to your group and competing with another group is an essential and primal experience for men, even if nowadays it's a darts team or a beekeeping club.

Pubs and beer. This is shorthand for 'companionship and conviviality'. It may seem Anglo-centric, but pubs – whether you visit them or not – have a strong appeal for most men. And as a social institution for discussion, amusement and relaxation (and beer) the pub has few rivals.

All men have a mix of these triggers, so the aim is to find a hobby that appeals to your particular mix.

Getting your wife on board

Inexplicably, women are liable to regard a man's new hobby as a childish and expensive waste of time. And don't kid yourself – she will spot straight away what you're up to. You think you have been subtly dropping hints into the conversation, but to her they register like 1,000 ton depth charges. For example:

- 'Did you know that John's taken up bee-keeping?'

- 'I was clearing out the garage and found my old fishing stuff / darts / easel / drum kit.'

- Did you read about that chap who found a hoard of treasure buried in a field?

- 'Apparently a goat can give 4 pints of milk a day. Amazing, isn't it?'

The warning signals could not be clearer – he's thinking of starting a hobby.

Your other half's attitude is likely to be that a hobby is better than having an affair, although if she weighs it up, there isn't a lot of difference, as this table explains:

Pros	Hobby	Affair
Gets him out of the house for long periods	Yes	Yes
He's pathetically grateful if I tolerate it	Yes	Yes
I can use it for bargaining purposes	Yes	Yes
Cons	Hobby	Affair
Liable to make the neighbours talk	Yes	Yes
Puts a strain on the household budget	Yes	Yes
He could dump me for it	No	Yes

Unbeknown to you, your wife will already have been calculating what she can get out of it. Marriage is a balancing act, and your new hobby is about to add a huge weight on to your side of the scales. She will be thinking of holidays, spa treatments, shopping trips, lunches with friends, new shoes, gym subscriptions, fancy restaurants, theatre tickets, or whatever else she may enjoy that will expensively redress the balance.

The minute you start your new hobby, be ready to hear this:

- 'What am I supposed to do while you're out playing darts/golf/fishing/art/archaeology?'

- 'Well, I'm off up to town. Didn't I mention I'm meeting the girls for lunch?'

- 'It's only fair. You need a new hobby, I need new shoes.'

The logic of this last one is beyond us, of course – she's got plenty of shoes. But we have been married long enough by now to know to keep quiet. The positive payoff for you is that there is no need to feel too much guilt about your new hobby.

What sort of hobbyist are you?

Be careful: how you handle hobbies says rather more about you than you'd care to reveal. If you take up one hobby and stick to it, chances are you're the strong and faithful type. If you flit between one hobby and the next, and your cupboards are full of the remnants of old ones, it suggest you may have once played the field, or at least must have been a terrible flirt.

If your wife is reading: there is no scientific evidence for this – it's just a theory. In fact the whole idea is absurd.

Pros and cons of some popular hobbies

Golf

Golf may be 'a good walk spoiled', as Mark Twain observed. But it's also the perfect excuse to get away from home for long periods of time, catch up with friends, and have a convivial drink afterwards. You don't have to dress up or travel for miles to do it, too. And you can claim the exercise is good for you, while being gentle enough not to make you sweat. The gadget aspect is positive, too, especially new clubs.

Pros

- Gets you out in the open air
- Can meet your friends and have a drink
- Provides moderate physical exercise
- An excuse to be away from home all day
- Satisfying to really whack a ball hard.

Cons

- The equipment isn't cheap

- Takes ages, and vast practice, to be any good

- Need good hand/eye co-ordination

- You might meet your boss on the course

- All that swinging can't be good for your back.

Risks of the game: Your wife may want to join you.

Famous golfers: Humphrey Bogart, Fred Astaire

Fly fishing

Fishing is a boyhood sport that we tend to give up in teenage years, when girls suddenly start to look more attractive than fish. Many of us return to it in our mature years, hopefully not for the opposite reason. The great thing about fishing is that you can take a break, and even lie down on the bank for a snooze, at any time during the day. This is less easy with golf.

Of all the different ways to fish, fly fishing is the only one that lets you put on waders and stand in the middle of a river – something almost all men will want to do from time to time. And it can take you to wild remote places, generally without your family. It doesn't have to be a loner sport; a day or weekend spent fishing with friends can be a re-creation of the good old days, including pubs. It appeals to the hunter-gatherer in us, even if you don't actually catch anything. And there are gadgets, from titanium reels to carbon-fibre rods. Tick, tick, tick those boxes!

Pros

- Gets you out in the open air
- Can meet your friends and have a drink
- Provides moderate physical exercise
- An excuse to be away from home all day
- Satisfying to catch a lively trout.

Cons

- The equipment isn't cheap
- Takes ages, and vast practice, to be any good
- Need good hand/eye co-ordination
- You might meet your boss on the riverbank
- All that casting can't be good for your back.

Risks of the game: You may fall in and drown.

Famous fly-fishers: Henry Winkler (the Fonz), Eric Clapton.

Darts

A tricky one to get away with. Since it mainly takes place in pubs, your wife will assume you just want an excuse to visit the pub regularly. Beware the counter-offer to buy you a dartboard so you can play at home; this will be useful for practice, of course, but it's the *social* benefit of darts that appeals to you, isn't it.

The sport of darts has acquired a professional air in the last 20 years in the UK and is regularly featured on television. So you can claim that you got the idea from watching it on the telly. Also emphasise that it's a team sport and will improve your social life and get you out of the house. Or, on a desperate note, that it is a richly historic game, one started by medieval archers, and you feel inspired to keep the tradition alive. (Best of luck with all those.)

Pros

- Gets you into the pub regularly. This alone is a massive result

- Can meet your friends and have a drink

- All that maths is good mental exercise

- An excuse to be away from home for an evening

- Satisfying to get a triple or bull.

Cons

- Pubs with dartboards can often be new, loud and horrible

- Takes ages, and vast practice, to be any good

- All that maths is hard work, and you'll look stupid if you regularly get it wrong

- You might meet your teenage children in the pub

- All that beer can't be good for you.

Risks of the game: dart-related injuries are common.

Famous darts players: Martin Amis, William Tell.

Keeping goats

Goat's milk is healthy, with no added hormones or other nasties. It can safely be consumed by the surprisingly large number of people with an allergy to cow's milk. Goats are very hardy creatures and will eat anything, including household scraps, garden rubbish and the contents of your neighbours' flower beds. Children love goats. Goat meat is low in fat and makes a fantastic Caribbean curry (just don't tell the children where it came from).

Pros

- Gets you out in the open air

- Saves you money on milk

- Chasing escaped goats is excellent physical exercise

- An excuse to get out into nature for long periods

- Satisfying to drink tea with your own goat's milk.

Cons

- Likely to be inconveniently close to home

- Costs a lot to get started

- Like pets, someone has to look after them when you're away

- Goats will eat your flowers and vegetables, and everyone else's

- All that bending over to milk them can't be good for your back.

Risks of the game: goats can bite and kick.

Famous goat-keepers: George Orwell, Marie Antoinette.

Why not invent a new hobby?

If existing hobbies don't appeal to you, why not start your own? If I had enough time I would like to try **Flyspotting**. There are dozens of types of fly to find, from common houseflies to now-rare horseflies, tiny fruit flies and yellow-and-black hoverflies. This would be a science-based hobby that gets you out in the open air. And the satisfying 'thwack' of your collecting book on each new specimen would add the element of hunter-gatherering, too.

Teaching an old dog new tricks

A new hobby can be hard work. You are mastering a new skill, and as we are all told, this gets harder with age. But does it, really? If you think back to childhood, the scene is littered with items thrown to the ground in tears of frustration: cricket bats, tennis rackets, musical instruments[2], maths textbooks, and Jane Austen novels, to name just a few.

In the prime of life, although your fingers fumble, your knees ache, and your memory features some alarming blank spots, you do have some blessed advantages over the young:

---

[2] Except pianos, although they deserved it the most

Patience. It doesn't have to be done today. You will get there. You know that sleeping on it may lead to a solution. (In fact, why not try that right now?)

Not trying to impress anyone. It's just a bit of fun, so who cares? But pick your golfing, fishing, etc. partners with caution – they shouldn't be too good, or your competitive trigger will be activated and your hobby will become the last thing it should be, work.

Pragmatism. You spurn perfectionism, knowing the value of short cuts, quick and dirty solutions, and staying focused on the goal rather than the technique (hello, ladies!). Your golf swing may look horrendous, your garden shed may be a botch-job, but they are good enough.

Cunning. If you want to cheat once in a while, why not? A ball chucked from the rough onto the fairway, a trout or some vegetables purchased in the supermarket and disguised as your own – it may occasionally be necessary, and you're ready to do it.

PK MUNROE

Cautionary tale of a new hobby - blogging

Everyone with a computer and half an opinion is at it these days. It's so easy to start blogging, but then you have to keep feeding the beast, week after week. It looks like a hobby, but in reality you have a demanding online pet.

How it starts

Other people's blogs look such fun, and it must be so interesting to do - why don't I get one? In a few clicks you can select a name for your blog, then spend some enjoyable hours playing with what it should look like, trying out different styles and colours.

In the first few weeks your blog is good, full of life. You fill it with all your bottled-up thoughts and opinions. You tell all your friends. You receive some compliments. You're inspired to write more, to start Tweeting and experimenting with other social media. You post photos (a sure route to spending much more money than is sensible on a new camera). You think about starting a second blog on a subject of particular interest to you. Who knows where this could lead? Maybe you could even make half a living at it?

But don't be tempted to share these thoughts. You will gradually realise that bloggers don't make money. People do it for fun, self-aggrandisement, because they believe it matters, or it's part of their career. Without strong motivators like these, a blog is likely to be fed at increasingly longer intervals, and with thinner material. It's not long before the wretched thing starts to nag away at its owner. What are you going to give the damn blog this time?

The last post

Which is why the internet is so distressingly littered with the corpses of dead blogs. You can tell them when you visit by the eerie stillness, and the date of the most recent post, several years ago. That last post feels like a gravestone, sometimes with a little note added to say that the owner has gone away, given up. It's sad. And interestingly there are more dead blogs around that were owned by men. Clearly women are either more persistent, or talkative, or better at burying their mistakes.

So men, remember the routine when a hobby dies - you stash all the equipment in the far corner of the cupboard under the stairs, and never mention it again. The online equivalent is to delete your dead blog. You can always say, when the subject comes up, 'Oh yes, blogging – I used to do that', like a digital old hand.

Could I give up my job and do this instead?

When you really get going on a hobby that's interesting and engaging, at some point you'll ask this question. Here are some examples of how the idea starts to ping around in your brain:

- If I grow most of our vegetables, we won't need to spend nearly as much on food, so we can get along on a much lower income, can't we? (Gardening)

- Nobody else around here is doing this. The milk and the meat is healthy – I can sell it at the market and make a living, can't I? (Goat-keeping)

- Some blogs make money. All it takes is a bit of luck, recognition from someone well known, and then it'll be easy money, won't it? (Blogging).

The answer to all these questions, I'm afraid, is no.

The hobby conundrum

Yes, some people make a living from an activity that started as a hobby. And some of them boldly claim to be 'doing something they love', and exhort us to join them, as if they have achieved a higher state of existence that the rest of us can only dream about.

They are deluded, of course. What once was their much-loved hobby has become their work. And if you listen carefully, there is a note of desperation in their claims, as if they are choking back thoughts of complicated tax returns and admin at midnight.

The fact is that any activity, once we have become dependent on it for a living, ceases to be simply a pleasure. Doubts start appearing in the back of the mind: What if I lose my ability? What if some young smartass comes in and does it better and cheaper than me? What if the business dries up? You know, or can imagine, the list.

The reason you enjoy a hobby so much is because it *isn't* a job. If you had to do it full time, and if you depended on it for income, you would start to dislike it, resent it, wish you could be doing something else, and thinking up ways to avoid it, just like real work.

What's going on with my body?

If, as scientists say, your body is just a sophisticated computer, in your fifties it starts to send out some alarming error messages:

Baldness. Ok, so we're going bald on top (and if not, you ought to be by now.) But what about losing hair in other places? Why does the hair on our shins, underarms, even forearms, start disappearing? Whose idea was that, and what is the point? There can hardly be an evolutionary reason, unless it's to help us swim faster as we get older. Is this some part of 'male pattern baldness' they didn't tell us about? It's a disquieting phenomenon, like a reverse adolescence.

Meanwhile your **ears and nostrils** are sprouting frenzied new hair growth. If only we could use if somewhere. Perhaps braided out of the ears up to the head for a frizzy comb-over, and swept out of the nose for a rather unstable moustache?

Appendages like your ears and nose, and fingers, seem to get larger (however not the appendage you wouldn't mind getting larger). The elephant ears are no joke – it's amazing how many mobile phone calls are terminated by the hard outer edge of the mature gent's ear pressing the 'End call' button. Surely a solution can be found? A large but discreet elastic band to press the ears to the head, maybe, or a tiny cotton cap for the ear tips?

That's enough – it's too depressing. Let's think about something more cheerful, or just stick our fingers in our ears (assuming they still fit) and sing LA LA LA.

Oh yes, **tripping over in the street.** Or even at home – how can one trip over when going up the stairs?

The truth about baldness

Incidentally, on the subject of baldness, young men who suffer the social agonies of going bald much too early may take comfort from the explanation that it's caused by an excess of the male hormone, testosterone, in their body.

Which, grasping at straws, can be translated as 'having an excess of maleness'. This feels like some form of compensation, or at least it would do if only anyone else could be persuaded on this point, or even took any notice of your efforts to drop it casually into the conversation.

And now here we are in our fifties, and most other men are bald too. This is a plague which, let's be honest, we early-adopters have looked forward to with some enthusiasm for a long time.

Except that, hang on, all these other blokes now going bald can't suddenly be acquiring a ton more of male hormones now, can they? So that theory was a load of bull, then. (Sigh.)

Filling out, or up

You've probably been waiting for me to mention getting fat. And that's all it deserves – a mention. Everyone has heard that in certain African (or is it Asian?) tribes, great respect is given to fat men, and to elders. This is the kind of information that makes you hoot in disbelief when young, but seems entirely fair and reasonable once in your fifties.

Except that nobody around us seems to feel the same way. Western society tells us we must be slim, energetic and youthful, as if all those years of excellent dinners, pies, chips, and vats of beer and wine can simply be wished away. And we've been brainwashed too – when meeting friends, we look hopefully for signs that they are fatter than we are, so we can tease them about it.

Personally I haven't the energy, but if anyone else wants to start a 'Respect for fat older people' campaign, I will certainly join up. And remember, it's not fat, it's bulk. It's 'putting on some weight'.

And if you are one of those annoying oldies who stays as slim as you were in your fifties, time to see your doctor – surely you must be suffering from an anxiety disorder, over-exercising, and other serious problems?

Don't look

The guaranteed solution to all these depressing things happening to your body is to carefully avoid paying attention to them. Never, ever look at yourself in a full-length bathroom mirror, and outside the bathroom, keep as many of your clothes on as possible. This includes poolside and while swimming (thus sadly negating that one benefit of losing bodily hair).

When you think about it, one's physical appearance is a good reason to avoid having a fling, which is allegedly one of the pitfalls of this time of life. I mean really, how are you going to carry that off, you porker?

Health

So now the aches and pains have started to arrive in earnest. Needless to say these should be shared extremely frugally with your other half.

Don't forget that women feel they are given the lifelong short straw when it comes to enduring regular bodily pain. They consider that most men don't know what pain is – we are wimps at best, whining hypochondriacs at worst.

She also doesn't want to be reminded of the passage of time affecting her, either. Increasing evidence that she is 'married to an oldie' is guaranteed to make her miserable, and cranky, and take it out on you.

So reserve your complaints for your get-togethers with male friends, who will be naturally sympathetic *and* want to make a joke of it, which is a pleasant combination.

And as you clutch your chest in alarm at that jabbing sensation that may just be indigestion,[3] go easy on the drama. Women have a vivid imagination, and now we are getting on (a bit), if she sees you doing this she is

---

[3] Or not. Don't quote me.

likely to think at least one of these things, or possibly all at once (how is that done?):

- He's got indigestion, the pig

- He's going to die and how will we cope then?

- He's going to die and I'll be left on the shelf, a poor widow past my prime, the bastard!

- Is he insured?

Exercise

Not that long ago, taking regular exercise was reserved for professional athletes and invalids. Now we are all at it.

There is something fundamentally sad about men in their fifties and older taking exercise. At the gym, in the pool, or pounding the streets – that grimly determined expression, the grunts, those ropy thighs and arms, all say "I don't want to be doing this." It's not just painful, it's embarrassing. Nobody over 50 really wants to be regularly found in shorts or swimming trunks.

I'm talking here about formal exercise, the kind you have to change into special clothes for. There's no harm in a spot of running in the park after the dog, or trotting to catch a bus, providing you pace yourself and have a good sit-down afterwards. But when you have to get into shorts or trunks, you are taking it all way too seriously[4].

---

[4] If you're one of those beefy, bones-crushed-in-your-bare-hands athletic types, by the way, I don't mean you – I mean all the other blokes. You know, those ones.

The gym

When archaeologists from the future dig down to our times, the gym outbreak is going to puzzle them mightily. Imagine the scholarly arguments about the purpose of rooms full of bizarre equipment designed to inflict pain! Why did these suddenly appear in so many hotels, offices, and other buildings? Was there a fascist takeover, requiring a sudden growth in torture centres? Or did the population, perhaps influenced by the hugely bestselling book 'Fifty Shades of Grey', turn *en masse* to masochism?

'What were they thinking of?' is likely to be the archeologists' baffled conclusion. Which sounds about right to me. What are we thinking of? Doesn't it occur to grim gym fanatics that it would be a lot easier to just get a job involving physical labour, rather than sitting in an office all day and then pounding the treadmill in the evening and at weekends?

When you think about it, there must be more going on than just a wish to shake off the fat. Possibly a desperate effort to stay young? Or a ruse to get away from the family? More likely, it's because everyone keeps banging on about how exercise is good for us.

But is it, really?

The exercise conundrum

Something is not right here. Medical experts tell us that as we get older our joints start to wear out, cartilage shrinks, bones become more brittle, and other fun things. If you need proof, look at professional athletes in their fifties – many of them can hardly walk. (However to balance things up, some of them can instead have a lie-down in their luxury yachts.)

But in the same breath the medical profession tells us how important it is to take more regular and vigorous exercise – which must make everything wear out even faster, mustn't it?

So the logic is that we exercise, making bones ache and knees stiffen for the sake of a healthy heart and lungs. Or to be scientific, we sacrifice our musculoskeletal system for the sake of our cardiovascular one. Is this a good exchange, one wonders? And is the sacrifice really necessary?

Other types of exercise

What if there is another way to get the blood pumping round our system, as we work up a sweat? Yes, I'm talking about:

- Watching sex and horror films with the lights off

- Repeatedly going on the scariest rollercoaster at amusement parks

- Taking part in chilli-eating contests

- Reading about the tax avoidance habits and luxurious lifestyles of the obscenely wealthy

- Listening to idiotic and highly-paid 'celebrities' being interviewed.

A regular program of this type of 'exercise' must get the blood coursing around the body and provide the cardiovascular system with a good workout, I'm sure doctors would agree. Why not ask yours? (Your wife might want some official proof that you need to perform the first three of these activities, so best to ask for a prescription.)

And in between these armchair workouts you can do a bit of light gardening, or play table tennis or darts, to keep things moving around without battering your bones. Or fishing, or golf. You could even try cycling to the pub, thus making a virtue out of a pleasure.

Sport

What the hell has happened to sports? We used to call them 'pastimes', pleasant activities to refresh ourselves, carried out with friends and colleagues, perhaps needing a bit of skill but done mainly for fun. Not any more. Sport and exercise are now hard to tell apart.

Here are some of the phrases associated with old and new concepts of sport:

Then	Now
Bit of a warm up	Cross training
Take it easy	Push your limits
Not so bad	Personal best
Let's go to the pub	Let's keep going

Sport nowadays is likely to be nasty, brutish and solo. It's intensely hard work, accompanied by punching the air, sweating, grunting, and roaring like a primate – lawn bowls is just not the same these days.

It's strange how nobody pokes fun at sporting activity. Take cycling – when did that stop being an enjoyable way to meander along, and turn into a high-speed chase? Those ridiculous aerodynamic hats, shaved legs, pencil-thin 'riders' on starvation diets, like jockeys – how crazed can you get? Why is there a crowd, and why aren't they all laughing?[5]

And all the accompanying nutrition nonsense – sports drinks, energy bars, vitamin shakes, power boosters. Who are they kidding? Everyone, apparently. Sport + Health = big money. But the multi-nationals don't invent new trends, they just follow along, picking up coins.

My theory is that sport has become the new religion:

Religion's goals	Sport's goals
Better	Fitter
Moral strength	Strength
Look after others	Look after me
Prepare to meet one's maker	Stay alive as long as possible

Modern sport is no activity for the manopause. I say bring back village cricket, social club snooker, rounders in the park, darts in the pub, tiddlywinks at home (surprisingly technical), beach football, and ping pong.

---

[5] When talking to a cycling fanatic, make sure you ask about their 'pushbike'.

Food

Everyone worries about an obesity epidemic in the western world, fretting about how it happened[6] and how to solve the problem[7]. But there is an important principle here: the ridiculous gap between the food we want, and what we are told is healthy:

We want	Is healthy
Pie and chips	Salad
Steak and chips	Mackerel and salad
Fried egg, bacon, chips, and beans	Poached egg on toast (no butter)
Pudding with cream and custard	Fruit
Beer and wine	Water

The question is: Why does all this unhealthy food exist? How did pies, chips and so on come into being, if they are so bad for us? What makes them so popular?

---

[6] pizza

[7] stop eating pizza

Why isn't it intensely satisfying to eat lettuce and raw vegetables, since they are so good for us and just what our body needs? What is it about the aroma of frying sausages that makes us salivate so? Shouldn't we automatically prefer and choose foods that are healthy and nutritious, like the animals do?

Of course anyone who has seen a suburban fox rummaging in the garbage knows that animals prefer unhealthy food when they can get it. That fox is hunting for leftover burgers and chicken nuggets – so much nicer and easier than catching voles and rabbits! But since those goodies are man-made, the argument still stands.

The food conundrum

It seems fundamentally wrong that the human body is harmed by the foods we crave. Evolutionarily speaking, it doesn't make sense. We should hunger for the foods our bodies need.

I think the answer is that our ancestors lived mainly on the dull and worthy stuff, like roots, grubs and berries, and only enjoyed a fry-up every now and then. They craved the flavour of meat and fat, while not getting enough to do them harm. And they had to work hard to get it – lots of running and spear-throwing.

A few thousand years of going on like this, and the craving for sausages was embedded deep into the human genome.

Those clever French

The French have an interesting take on salad. You have to eat the salad leaves, but they are dotted with more alluring items like chunks of sausage, chicken or blue cheese. Those winning combinations mean you can claim to take in a lot of salad while hovering up the bad foods you enjoy.

Why aren't the scientists working full-time on creating artificial sprays with the genuine odour and taste of frying food? There is a fortune to be made here. Food manufacturers already have chemists who, fiddling around with plant genes, can artificially create a scent of strawberries and other fruit that is so realistic, you can't believe it's not genuine. So I am confidently expecting a new range of salad sprays for lettuce leaves that add the authentic flavour and aroma of sausages, chips, bacon and pies. (Of course you'd have to eat with your eyes shut.)

New-style supermarkets needed

Although we need to eat less fat, we are able to get hold of it all the time, every day. My solution is simple: Hunter-gatherer supermarkets. These would be for men only, featuring:

- A magnetic-tipped spear for each male shopper to pull tinned food off the shelves, and to impale items from the meat counter

- Shopping baskets made from woven reeds

- Grasses, bushes and trees placed throughout the store

- Ambient jungle sounds (roaring lions, exotic bird calls, howler monkeys) played over the loudspeaker system

- Traps and hazards in the aisles to increase the sense of danger

- Embedded animal paw-prints in the floor tiles to encourage tracking

- Caches of fruit and vegetables hidden in unexpected places

- Hand nets to catch live fish, crabs and shrimp at the seafood counter.

In this way men in particular would have a workout to put together the evening meal. And it would be a lot of fun, too.[8]

---

[8] The reader of my book 'The Thursday Night Letters' may recognise this list from a marketing proposal I sent to the chairman of Morrison's supermarkets (rejected).

The booze

By now we have learned a thing or two, usually the hard way.

Wine

Red wine is beneficial for your heart, they say, although it seems every time you open a newspaper this claim is either (a) refuted as an incorrect interpretation of the research, or (b) supported by new research.

If you were a beer-drinker as a young man, it can be hard work to just sip wine, rather than glug it down.

Have you noticed how strong wine is getting? A 12% red used to be a lucky find. Then suddenly 13% ones were common, maybe due to the popularity of Australian wine. This started a strength war, so that 14% and 14.5% are all over the place, and now wines weighing in at 15% are not so unusual, which is getting close to the strength of sherry or port. Nasty. They must add sugar and shake it up to reach that volume of alcohol. Two glasses of one of these big, dense, dark reds will give you a zombie buzz, and a cruel headache next day.

Go to southern Europe and they've got the right idea – nice weak whites and reds you can quaff back in the sunshine like a teenager, with no ill effects.

Beer

Beer just keeps getting better, with little breweries springing up to provide a greater range of good stuff than ever before. Where were they in our young years, when 'Double Diamond' was touted as a quality bitter?

Drinking lager with curry, as every curry house encourages you to do, makes you feel incredibly bloated – it's the reaction of all that rice to all that beer. Red wine is what you need here.

And the rest

Whisky, which used to be so vile to our young tastebuds, is now rather good. It appeals to the mature palate, one that has probably been worn away by all the bad stuff we've been eating and drinking for 40+ years. We now understand why so many old buffers in our youth liked whisky so much.

Spirits with juice are for teenagers, tasting like sugary drinks. Bitter mixers work better – lemon, tonic, etc.

But we are also getting used to some unwelcome facts:

- **Red wine** makes you as fat as a pig, and because it is so strong these days, will give you a filthy hangover too

- **Drinking beer** makes you as fat as a two pigs. And although we no longer have room for more than 3 pints, these appear to add the same bulk as 5 or 6 did in our young days

- **Whisky is the devil's brew** – more than a couple of small glasses and you'll have a Grim Reaper of a hangover, and a vague memory of having started several fights

- **Spirits** mixed with anything get you drunk insanely fast.

The only sensible thing is to drink a modest amount of not-very-strong beer, or white wine. (Or nothing, if you like the sound of that.)

Hangovers

A lot of talk is heard about hangovers getting less noticeable with age. Sheer nonsense, of course. The truth is that the morning after six pints of beer as a young man is pretty much the way you feel now after two-thirds of a bottle of red wine.

And since you are a lot more likely now to have a responsible job, this adds pain to your weekday wine-drinking headache.

All deeply unfair, but there it is.

THE MANOPAUSE MANUAL

Pubs and socialising

It is hard to beat Dr Johnson on this subject:

"There is nothing which has yet been contrived by man, by which so much happiness is produced as a good tavern or inn."

The pub conundrum

It seems that as a young man there was little or nothing to keep you out of a pub – any pub – but in one's fifties, despite having a very discerning sense of what makes for a good pub, you are much less frequently found inside one.

If your friends are also married, some even with children, getting away for an evening in the pub appears to be a remote prospect. If you do push for a visit, it rapidly shapes up into a major event requiring complicated arrangements. Debt will start to subtly accrue on your side of the marital weighing-scales, to be balanced out in future with plenty of activities you won't enjoy.

Or else our wives want to come along too – which is fine, of course! But it's not somehow the same as getting together with the 'lads'.

The pub is no longer the natural place to regularly congregate and socialise. A casual 'See you down the pub' has now turned into a system of turn-taking in hosting meals at one's home (these can be called 'dinners' but never 'dinner parties' in my rule book), arranged weeks in advance, and generally not organised by you.

It would not happen like this if men were in charge. We would simply say 'Curry house, Saturday?' and the thing would be done. No cooking, no washing up, too much hot food and strong red wine – perfect.

How to get out to the pub again

If you have kept up your friendships with men your own age, and some of them live in your town/city/county, this should be fairly easy to orchestrate.

If you have let your friendships lapse, a bad mistake but a surprisingly common one among married men, you have some preparation to do. Start finding out who among the old gang still lives in your area, and get emailing or phoning in an effort to rebuild a small group of chaps you get on with. You may well be surprised to find your wife is supportive of these efforts

– but when you think about it, male friends are a lot less threatening than the alternative.

And on this simple fact lies the solution to getting yourself out to the pub again, and doing so *regularly*. As described in earlier chapters on hobbies, the key is to create a small beachhead, and gradually reinforce it over time until it has become an unalterable part of the social landscape. Here's a good starting point:

> *"Fred has asked me and Jim out to The Feathers on Thursday night for a pint – his wife is away and he thought it would be nice for the old gang to get together."*

There are several important aspects to this innocent-seeming suggestion:

- Firstly, you know that your wife finds Fred or Jim (preferably both) a bit boring / boisterous / annoyingly flirtatious / hobby-obsessed, etc.

- The Feathers is a rather unappetising pub, grubby and with no food except crisps

- 'His wife is away' implies that this is a one-off, or at least very irregular event, *and* that wives won't be there

- *'for a pint'* creates an image of blokes standing in a group holding pint glasses

- Thursday is a weekday. Don't even try to do this on a weekend.

Whatever you do, don't come home late or drunk. Make it clear that the couple of hours in the pub were simply about socialising with your pals. You want to establish this as being entirely separate from bad behaviour in your dissolute youth.

When your wife asks how it went, be sure to play it down. 'Not bad' is one of those useful phrases so maddening to our other halves, being both brief and lacking all information. You don't want to give the impression it was a big deal for you. But to make sure your wife labels such events as not her thing, mention that there was quite a lot of conversation about railway engines, or so-and-so's new hobby of collecting lichens.

Making it regular

On this initial outing to the pub, part of the conversation should have been about how to get out more often. If at least a couple of your wives could start a hobby that consumed an evening, this would be a perfect way in:

> "Julie [Fred's wife] is doing her choir practice on Thursday so he's asked me and Jim out for a pint after supper."

And now is the time to plant suggestions about activities your wife could do. Singing in the choir is all the rage at the moment, but even if your wife can't hold a tune in a basket, there is always textile-weaving, pottery, learning Spanish, calligraphy, DIY tattooing, or any number of harmless activities. Pick up a few brochures when you happen to be passing the local library and leave them lying around artlessly at home.

Your goal

Keep up the momentum and within a year you could be visiting the pub once a month, twice a month, or even – the golden goal attained by the very few – every week!

And remember, by this time it will gradually have become an essential part of your social landscape, just like your chosen hobby.

'But what did you talk about?'

Once your pub visit with the lads has become accepted, get ready to regularly hear this question from your other half. To her it seems perfectly reasonable – after all you have been out with friends and you must have something to report. If a group of women friends went out to the pub, they would come back with enough material to write a short novel.

Chances are that you spent the evening discussing knotty matters such as why no publisher has yet come up with a glossy magazine for criminals, or how come the streets fill up with attractive women only in the summer months, or why there isn't a national lottery where the winner joins the Royal Family for a week, or how to design a gadget that will easily and quickly mend the holes that keep appearing in the toes of your socks.

Naturally you are uneasy about sharing these discussions with your other half, and are reduced to saying 'oh you know, this and that' or 'nothing much' which will merely inflame her irritation, and convince her that all men become imbeciles over time. Which is just about where you want her.

Putting the world to rights

It's perhaps to be expected that as we attain our maturer years, men see more clearly exactly what is wrong with everything – and how to put it right. (Although it's odd that women don't seem to reach the same level of clear-sightedness, or spend time thinking how to solve important issues.)

This kind of problem identifying and solving ability is perhaps a 'male thing', related to our being drawn to hammers, screwdrivers and power tools, more or less since birth. Clearly our genes are telling us to get out there and fix things.

So in our glorious fifties we find the perfect match of a deep understanding of what isn't working properly with the world, and the way to fix it. Interestingly this is less about finding solutions to abstract problems, such as:

- World peace
- Human aggression and territoriality
- Economic inequality
- Environmental despoliation
- Species depletion

It's not that we don't care about these things, but better minds than ours are already working on them.

We tend to focus more on specific problems and how to find lasting solutions, including:

- People who talk too loudly on mobile phones (Solution: invent a gadget that you can point at them to disrupt their signal, and possibly deliver a small but painful shock, too)

- Young people who play their music too loud, late into the night (Invent a gadget you can point at them to zap their bloody noise, while trying not to remember that thirty years ago you were keeping people awake with some pretty dire music, though surely not as bad as this racket)

- Pubs with televisions or music playing at too loud a volume (Invent a gadget that – hang on a minute, possibly combine all these gadgets into one handset!)

And so forth. These are real, concrete concerns, requiring carefully thought-out solutions. And as you reach maturity, literally dozens of issues like this will come to your attention, each requiring urgent work.

Finding a solution to just one of these could propel you to fame and riches. Here's one example: where is the device to rapidly and easily mend a hole in a sock, created by our ever-hardening toenails? Something clever like a cotton-stapler, perhaps. Now how would that work? And off we go, improving the world one problem at a time.

'Grumpy old men'

Strangely, our other halves tend to become positively bored with these topics that are so important and fascinating to us. Make a few critical comments about mobile phone use in the street ('why is he shouting?'), or modern music (so much worse than heavy acid rock or punk) or other modern annoyances, and before long our wives start to snap at us.

They seem to think we are becoming 'Grumpy old men' as the popular stereotype has it – although anyone who has watched those TV programmes or read the books of the same name can only nod enthusiastically at their perceptive identification of multitudes of problems, coupled with clever solutions.

Of course what really bothers your wife is that if you are at risk of being seen to be a grumpy old man, this is somehow a reflection on her stage of life – and our partners do not want the word 'old' coming anywhere near them.

Putting the world to right in pubs

So where better to discuss and solve these matters than in the pub with your friends? This is surely what beer was invented for. Indeed you may have found even in your youth that discussions in pubs focused on what was wrong with the world and how to solve it, although this may have tended towards suitable gadgets to make girls fancy you, or at least remove their clothes (that sort of thing).

And the sure way to get your other half positively pushing you out to the pub is to start pontificating (I mean, problem-solving) at home, preferably during an evening meal.

How not to be a grumpy old man

We have established that the label 'grumpy old men' is badly misapplied to chaps in their fifties engaging in identifying and solving problems. However, we have to admit that at some stage – maybe in their seventies or eighties – some men can start to focus on complaining about things, rather than finding solutions.

Not having reached this fine older age it's difficult to imagine what that must be like. But the best way to avoid being labelled a complaining curmudgeon is surely to adopt a Buddha-like serenity when faced with modern irritants. Here are some useful mantras for re-programming your brain:

Adverts are...

Not moronic and devious efforts to trick us out of our money. Remember they are prepared by creative people who live in fear of losing their jobs to even younger twats. Feel that serene pity!

Smartphones are...

Not a shiny gadget that steals our leisure time and turns us into zombies. Remember they come in very useful when you are trapped in a Swiss avalanche. See the good side!

Celebrities are...

Not unhinged egos on a stick. They are simple, hard-working entertainers who struggled heroically against the odds to get on the telly. Admire them!

Corporate conglomerates are...

Not psychotic tyrannies ruthlessly raping the planet to achieve world domination. They're just trying to give their shareholders a good time. That's so nice!

And so it goes on – I'm sure you can think of more mental gymnastics to take the edge off reality. There could even be a health benefit here – repeating these mantras may well help to reduce blood pressure, enabling you to carry on knitting far into your dotage.

Philosophy – nice in theory

At our time of life the consolations of philosophy can start to appeal. It's increasingly popular, with plenty of books and TV shows making the teachings of the great philosophers accessible to a general audience.

Men of a certain age are often advised to take note of the Stoic philosophers. Their ideas about cultivating fortitude and endurance start to make a lot of sense to chaps who may not after all be able to afford a sports car or grow a beard (see other chapters).

The Stoics recommend that when you're in a difficult spot, you should first figure out what you can and can't change about the situation – and ignore the latter.

Say you are out walking alone on the wild moors and get stuck in a dangerous mire, starting to sink above your boots. Here is an example of a Stoic analysis:

- Can I get out of the mire unaided? No.
- Is there anyone around? No.
- Is there a ladder to hand? No.
- Do I have a mobile phone? Yes, but the battery is dead.
- Conclusion: so am I.

But now you will be stoically calm about your fate, instead of uselessly thrashing around, yelling for help, cursing your stupidity, or trying to blame someone else ('she made me wear these heavy boots!').

All fine in theory. The only problem is that when you're actually in the middle of a crisis, rational thought jumps out of the window and the emotions grab the controls. We fight or we flee, we thrash around and yell, but it's a rare person indeed who can force their reason back into the driving seat.

And if such people do exist, they were born that way, with iron self-control. They didn't read a Stoic's philosophy book and suddenly change their nature.

Which brings us to a practical philosophy that doesn't expect any improvement from you. I call it 'tragic realism'. The phrases you need to learn are:

- Don't blame me, I was born this way.
- Nobody's perfect.
- I couldn't help myself.
- It's just the way I am.

And there is all the practical philosophy you need, in four simple expressions.

Fashion

Don't worry, there is very little to say on the subject of clothing. It's more a matter of what not to wear.

The jeans and t-shirts must die

In your heart of hearts you know that jeans and t-shirts are for the young. Yet so many of us continue to kid ourselves that this is a universal look, suitable for all ages. It's not.

If you're honest, you know that with the exception of a couple of Hollywood stars, men over 50 don't look right in jeans and t-shirts. After a certain age we just can't carry it off with any conviction. And imagine how annoying it would have been, as a young man discovering Levis, leather boots or Loon Pants, if your father's generation had started wearing them too. But this is what we're doing to today's youth, and it's just not right. An enlightened government would set on the spot fines for men over 50 wearing t-shirts and jeans.

How ironic that in our brief teenage years, when we were constantly aware of how awful/spotty/weedy we looked, we were in the perfect shape for jeans and t-shirts. They never looked better on us.

And why is that? For the simple but terrible reason that the place we used to hang our jeans has disappeared. Yes, the hip bone is no more. You now have two options for where to hitch your trousers, but neither of them is flattering:

You and your belt line

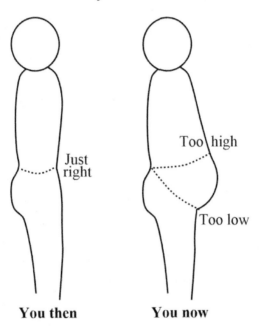

You then   **You now**

Of course the low-slung belt is very 'cool' now among youth. But it's not for us.

If not jeans and t-shirts, then what?

Something more comfortable and suited to our age group, of course. I'm not going to tell anyone what to wear, though. I'm certainly not going to mention corduroy trousers, or loose-fitting cotton shirts. Nor cardigans, buttoned or zippered, with pockets. Nor tweed. You can start your own trend, not copy mine. But whatever you wear, get a size too large. You won't regret it.

Can I still wear trainers?

If you must. But do you really need to? Can't you see that it's all part of a rather exhausting effort to feel young, even as you run out of puff from 10 minutes continuous walking, and find yourself regularly tripping over paving stones?

Get yourself some nice comfortable shoes. Soft leather or suede, that's the ticket. The right ones feel like you're wearing slippers, and you know what – that's a good feeling, isn't it?

Avoiding the deranged codger look

Some combinations that seem to be typically adopted by the oldies are best avoided:

- Shoes with white socks (especially drawn tight up the shin)

- Sandals with socks of any colour (this does feel comfortable, but you will see people crossing the road to avoid you)

- Trousers fastened tightly, high above the waist, with plenty of sock and bare leg on show.

Of course you should grow a beard

Beards are popular now, especially with the young. To a mature gent this is a useful trend, since our own efforts won't stand out so badly. Thanks, hipsters!

If you already have a beard, this chapter is not aimed at you. Obviously, you have managed to overcome the hurdles described here, so well done for that. But don't get smug about it. Your so-called 'ability' is just a matter of random fortune – a throw of the genetic dice.

Why grow a beard?

This is a surprisingly complex, subtle issue. Here are just some reasons you might want to have in mind when your wife is informed or becomes aware of your plan:

To grow hair where hair will grow. Those of us going or gone bald appreciate the argument that if I'm losing hair in one place, at least I can still grow it in another.

Because it looks good. Admittedly this applies to the kind of strong, manly beard that grows rapidly, rather than the slow, patchy, unruly, fifty shades of grey crop that some of us end up with.

It looks distinguished. A variant on 'It looks good', but with more female appeal. This line is especially worth trying if you are going grey on top. (Most men feel uneasy about the very idea of trying to look distinguished – does it mean we have to wear a bow tie? But now we have sufficient cunning to keep these thoughts to ourselves.)

It hides the blemishes. Those deepening lines, gaunt cheeks and scars will magically disappear under a beard, as will the strange marks and blotches (where did they come from?) that start to appear on men's faces after 50. Women should appreciate this argument, although they may regard the strategy as unfair. (But then we can't borrow their make-up and 'anti-ageing' cream, can we. Can we?)

To stick it to the boss. If you are in the kind of office job where the men typically don't wear beards, there is a deep appeal to grow one just to say 'up yours', however mildly, to the prevailing culture. In more conformist work environments a beard is like wearing jeans and sneakers to work, except that no-one can tell you off for it. Got to be worth a try. Don't tell your wife about this angle, though, as the look you receive will make you feel deeply sad and deluded at the same time.

It's natural. It seems wrong, going against nature, to shave off all that hair which is trying so hard to grow, day in and day out. Being clean-shaven is a pointless cultural affectation. Nature wants us to have a beard. And on an increasingly desperate note, it can't be good for me, or even I've got sensitive skin. (Does our skin grow thinner as we get older? Sounds plausible.)

To keep warm. As we get older we become more susceptible to cold winds, drafts, and winter generally. A scarf, a hat and a beard make a formidable barrier and help to keep us healthy. (Good one!)

To prevent sunburn on your face when deep-sea fishing off Cuba. This worked for Ernest Hemingway, so why not adapt it for your circumstances?

Because I can. A pleasing reason: it's something women and children can't do. So there – how do you like that? (Best keep this one to yourself.)

What's stopping you from growing a beard?

If men without beards are honest, the main reason is that it might not work. We have in our heads some iconic beard images: Hemingway's massive Father Christmas job, for example, Lenin's neat little pointy one, or Frank Zappa's luxuriant 'grumper'. If ours doesn't live up to those standards, people may laugh at us.

Of course it's absurd. What if we applied the same impossibly high standards to other areas of life? Because one cannot sing like Pavarotti or Paul

McCartney, does one therefore never sing, not even in the shower? Most of us don't resemble a film star but we still manage to have a love interest of some sort. So why the hell should our beards have to be like those of Hemingway, Lenin or Frank Zappa, who probably applied hair dye and had professionals to shape, massage and trim theirs, the effeminate twerps?

It is plain wrong and unmanly to allow such intimidating thoughts to prevent us from growing a perfectly respectable, if slightly scrappy and wayward beard. Look at Abraham Lincoln's scraggy one, and Steve Jobs's stubbly one. Many current thinkers consider Hemingway, Lenin and even Zappa to be over-rated, while the stock of Lincoln and Jobs has never been higher. Says it all, doesn't it?

How to grow a beard

You probably experimented with beard-growing as a young man, and maybe even grew a decent one if you were lucky. (It's just genes, remember. Random accident. Nothing to feel proud about.)

But that was a youthful trial. Now it's time for the real thing. And before you start, you must pluck up the courage to see it through. It's no good, and I speak with experience, 'giving it a try' for a few days to 'see if I like it'. This leaves the door wide open for your wife, children and beardless friends and workmates to pitch in and poke fun at your paltry growth. Next thing you know, it's gone – you got rid of it, but in reality it was shaved off for you by others.

During this difficult early period you could try feigning excessive passion and commitment, for example wearing a t-shirt or badge claiming "It's my body" (like women do) or "Reclaim The Chin". Got to be worth a try.

The beard barrier

Growing a beard takes nerve and stubbornness. You have to decide to go down that road, and just ignore everyone else and their unkind or witty remarks. So grit your teeth – and remember that for most of us, a proper beard takes several months to be recognisable as such. Think of it as a process of giving birth, if that helps, although it's unlikely people will offer you their seats on public transport while you gestate the thing.

Taking a holiday is a well-known method of getting started. But here's a tip: don't wait until day 1 of the holiday. Stop shaving as long as possible before the holiday has even begun – just pretend your razor broke, or something. This will give you valuable days of growth as a head start.

Trimming the unruly bits to create a slim beard-profile is a good way to reduce the level of comments and make people miss what you're up to. This is especially true of the neck, where you may get a good growth, in sad contrast to your chin. Generally speaking, anything that's visible half an inch below the jaw line when you look into the mirror should be ruthlessly removed.

The stealthy start allows you to suddenly spring your beard on the world, which is better than having people snigger as they watch it struggle to form. The trick is to gradually grow your sideburns longer and longer, a few millimetres at a time, until they are well below your earlobes – and at the same time leave an unshaven line along the tip of your chin, which can easily be mistaken for a natural shadow. Your expanding sideburns may attract sarcastic remarks about yokels, and queries about when you plan to start a tribute band for The Wurzels, but it's a small price to pay. Then, a day or two before a long weekend, stop shaving altogether, and encourage the stubble to start filling in the gaps.

Joining the French Foreign Legion is a little extreme, perhaps, but there you have a prime example of a group of men left in peace to grow a beard, and nobody starts criticising them for it when they eventually get back home.

Problems once you've got a beard

Your wife doesn't like it. Aside from a few exceptional women, you can be pretty sure this will be the case. Try saying "I can't go back, it's part of me now", making it sound like a hugely retrograde psychological step that will cause some unspecified damage to your personality. Funnily enough women may appreciate this argument, having experienced similar emotions themselves when considering a change of hairstyle, or even shoes.

It's itchy as hell. Beard-wearers will assure you that the itching goes away after a few years.

It hasn't grown properly. Give it more time – it will probably thicken, and the patchy bits will fill in. Only consider extreme solutions, such as hair transplants (eg. from the back of your head) if you are truly in crisis.

People remark on it. Think yourself lucky – back in the early 1900s, children in the street would shout "Beaver!" at anyone wearing a beard, and sometimes throw stones.

Reasons not to grow a beard

- It just hasn't grown properly. Mainly because your wife didn't give you enough time. She apparently doesn't understand that these things take years, not days

- People who are down and out have beards. It's true, just take a look. (Quite luxuriant ones, too – the swine!)

- It's uncivilised. Shaving, contrary to what the beardies tell you, is the mark of a civilised man

- It's completely pointless and not worth trying. So there.

Do I really need a sports car?

The sports car debate is the defining issue of the manopause. The whole idea of a man of 50-odd years driving a flashy two-seater is cruelly mocked by most of the population. Women smile knowingly, especially when terms like 'high performance' are used, and young men (rather traitorously, considering that their turn will come) jeer openly from the sidelines. What exactly is going on here? As usual, a seemingly simple issue turns out to have underlying complexities.

A man of mature years driving a sports car is often assumed to be trying to attract women. But is a sports car really a babe magnet? Can you seriously imagine waiting in traffic and having women come running up and asking for a ride? Not round my way, that's for sure. But it certainly is a bloke magnet – you are vastly more likely to get chaps enviously eyeing your machine. Which brings us to the first reason to want a sports car:

Showing off to other men. An expensive sports car is a massive status symbol, and having one puts you in the top 2% of your fellow males. It says 'I have enough disposable income to blow a big chunk on this unnecessary little runabout without caring'. Of course the driver may have re-mortgaged his home and taken up crime, or even gambling on the stock market, to fund his toy (and those of us looking on can certainly hope so), but that aspect is not on display. One purchase, and you are way ahead of the pack.

This is why so many younger men are so cruel and cutting about older chaps driving, say, a red Triumph two-seater. They desperately want but can't afford one themselves, and it's highly ironic since the young ones think they could make much better use of it. So they mock and jeer at the sad old gent as a figure of fun, trying to relive his youth and hugely kidding himself that he can still pull women. Sheer envy on their part. In fact you can add this to the list of reasons for wanting one.

Next motive: all that power under the bonnet expresses a yearning to get the hell away from it all, at top speed. So a sports car is:

A means of escape. Not forever of course. But I bet most men with a sports car prefer to go for a spin alone, so they can fantasise about roaring away to somewhere else, at least for a while. Which is why they find excuses not to take their wives along. I can hear them now:

> "I'd love you to come along darling, but I'm a bit worried about the [names obscure engine part]. It's been playing up and might blow / shear / crack / implode any time now. In fact I'm taking her to the mechanic later."

All lies, of course – and notice that the car ('her') is going to 'the mechanic' rather than 'the garage' where the rest of us take a car; such a special machine needing its own expert to work on it.

But the fact is that sports car owners have found a means to satisfy that craving we all have from time to time, to escape, get away, driving like a rocket (with a nice engine roar) down some new unexplored roads. Swine!

It's a cave. Car owners know that their car is more than a vehicle – it's a deeply personal space, a little home they carry around with them. (This is the explanation for road rage, which seems so wildly irrational until you understand that a primate is defending his home.) A family car must be shared, but your own sports car is your own cave, a place that belongs just to you.

All of the above applies to boats, too, in spades (which is the real reason they're so expensive). Babe magnet? Not really. Status symbol? You bet. Means of escape? Yes, and to just about anywhere. Cave? Yes, and on the water, putting you in touch with the wild. You can even go fishing! Tick, tick, tick those boxes!

How to get a sports car

Unless you are wealthy, it is going to involve a lot of deception, of yourself and others. Here are some useful starting positions to try on your nearest and dearest:

Wouldn't it be fun to have a sports car? No, really, wouldn't it? Just imagine us on a sunny morning whizzing down to the coast for the day, the wind in our hair!

This romantic appeal is a good enough place to start, although of course you have no intention of taking your wife out in it for more than twice a year, or for longer than half an hour. It's your car, not hers.

I've always wanted a sports car. Of course you have, you dope. You've also wanted a lot of other things your wife isn't necessarily aware of. But a wistful tone to your voice can work wonders here, suggesting that maybe you never will fulfil your dream, time is marching on, the cruel hand of fate could chop you down any day now...

It's surprising how cheap sports cars actually are. This is true, if you focus just on the purchase price of a fifth-hand, British-made, deeply unreliable and massively high-maintenance model (or, a potty little fibreglass kit-car that will do a top speed of 50 and blow away in a strong wind). The running costs will soon outstrip the price – 'classic' models are notorious drinkers of petrol and suffer more mechanical problems than even classic British motorbikes. But keep pointing to the purchase price and hope no-one in your family knows any better, while not thinking about the much lower resale price, or the fact that it will be losing value with each passing hour.

The downsides

Where to start?

The cost. Not just the purchase cost, but running costs – acquire anything but a new sports car (prohibitively expensive for most of us) and you are soon dealing with major engine problems, hunting down spares in unlikely areas of the country, and finding a specialised mechanic or garage, where they will be smiling and rubbing their hands as you drive up.

The takeover. Even if you have a very understanding family, they will demand to be taken lots of drives in your pride and joy, thus removing half the point of it. **The blame.** The minute there is any call for a large expense – a luxury holiday, say, or a nursing home for a parent – you will get the blame if it is no longer affordable.

The time. Just think of all those hours to be spent buffing the bodywork, removing rust from every bit of chrome, sourcing spare parts, and wondering what is causing the latest oil leak. The ratio of hours driving to hours spent fiddling must be tiny.

The opinion of others. Like it or not, you know people out there are pointing and sniggering, if only to themselves. This doesn't make you feel so great. It will niggle away at you, like the princess's pea under the mattress.

The alternatives

We've established that by acquiring a sports car (or a boat) you are ticking some important boxes for a man – it puts us at the head of the pack, gives us a means of escape and provides us with a cave of our own.

However the downsides are, for many of us, prohibitive. And if you're reading this book you are probably not the caveman type, ready to ignore the feelings of wife and family for a selfishly huge layout of savings on a shiny bauble that, ignore it or not, sets many people sniggering.

So instead of a sports car, why not consider getting a different type of cave? This opportunity is dealt with in the next chapter.

Me and my shed

The idea of a man owning a shed has become something of a joke in recent years. The book 'Men and Sheds' probably started it off (although if you read the book and look at the sensible pictures, it treats the subject with the correct amount of seriousness). Nevertheless it seems that nowadays you can't say the word 'shed' in public without setting off giggles, smirks or eye-rolling among women.

Actually this is all to the good. Because women think sheds are funny, it is quite easy to get one of your own without causing domestic alarm or resistance. It becomes a little joke that they will enjoy telling their female friends. Meanwhile you are busy ordering a big one – no less than 3 square metres if you can get away with it. Key points to consider:

- Site it as far away from the house as you can manage. No point in having your retreat within shouting distance.

- If you can put it somewhere else, like on an allotment, so much the better.

- Put a damn big lock on the door, to 'deter burglars', or more accurately, family members.

Furnishing your shed

Of course this is up to you and depends on your interests. Personally I wouldn't be without:

- a workbench and tools. If you are at all mechanically-minded (and most men are) you need to have close to hand tools like chisels, hammers, saws, drills, and so on. This helps you to justify saying to your family, when you retire to the shed for long periods: 'It's my workshop' or more specifically 'I've got to fix that thing'. Nothing much may come out of it, but that's not the point – you need the tools.

- bottles and jars in case I get the urge to make wine

- a bookcase

- playing cards

- dartboard

- shelves on which to put all those bits and pieces that get thrown out of the house, or at least complained about: fossils, shells, interesting stones, driftwood, old ships' nails, locks that need repairing, etc.

- a stack of old newspapers and magazines

- a bottle of something warming (sloe gin is ideal) and a couple of glasses / mugs for when your male friends drop round, as they certainly will

- pictures on the walls of apparently sub-standard artistic value, although I can't see what's wrong with them

- a cosy lamp (this means supplying electricity of course, although oil lamps could be worth trying)

- a regular chair, a few stools and a small but comfortable armchair.

You also need a restricted area for gardening tools, which were the alleged purpose of buying a shed in the first place. To make sure the garden tools don't take over your space, put up nails on the walls and ceiling where they can be wedged and hung (don't try this with a lawnmower, though).

Of course you can see what's happened here: you've created a cave. And a better one than a sports car – cheaper, less prone to rust, and certain to inspire some degree of envy from fellow-men who haven't got one.

An allotment is not a garden

This book offers zero advice on gardening. However in his fifties, earlier if possible, the British (and possibly European) male should start to think seriously about getting an allotment. The reasons are simple – it's like having a second home, it has a shed to play in, and you can grow a few vegetables too, which appeals to the deep-rooted hunter-gatherer in all of us.

Best of all you are likely to get some solitude. The idea of an allotment may not appeal to your family, if you paint them a suitably off-putting picture:

- Windy, exposed site
- Grotty shed
- Endless weeding
- Grimy, dull or dangerous chores to be done
- Smelly manure heaps
- Grumpy, eccentric neighbours
- Prevailing rain, cold, etc.

If you prefer companionship, you can share the allotment with a friend. Not only does this mean you get a hand with fixing up the shed, weeding, wheelbarrowing manure and battling with the grumpy neighbours, but if you play your cards right it can be another reason to keep your family off the plot. This is because it's not your allotment, it's shared with Fred, and you feel a bit uncomfortable inviting other people, don't you, since Fred can get a bit funny about that, can't he?

The best part of any allotment is the shed (see previous chapter). Get the biggest shed you can afford, otherwise you run the risk that there will only be room for the gardening tools, and nowhere to put armchairs, shelves, bottles, and so on.

No gardening tips here

Except for one: to grow crops that can be stored in the shed. Then, each time you come home from the allotment you can bring back a handful of onions, potatoes, garlic, dried beans, etc that have been hanging up in the shed for months. This allows you to visit the allotment and do basically no work – perhaps having a companionable game of cards or a drink instead – but still give your family the impression you've been hard at it.

The view from the wife

Of course none of this is really fooling your better half. She understands that the allotment is essentially an escape mechanism, a well-disguised skive, even if you do sometimes work quite hard there. Be ready for the occasional domestic row about this. Vegetables are cheap enough in the shops, as she will doubtless point out during one of those arguments about why this household chore hasn't been done, or that family outing arranged. To which, by the way, you must counter with:

- At least we know where my vegetables come from, not like those shiny fakes in the supermarket
- Gardening is good exercise for me
- It's so much better for the planet than buying supermarket 'French' beans from Kenya, in all that plastic packaging
- (at this point your wife has stopped paying attention, but keep going)
- My old-fashioned vegetable varieties are brimming with nutrients
- I can't let Fred do it all himself, can I?

Your longer-term goal is to insert the allotment concept into everyday family life. You want "I'm just off to the allotment" to sound as routine and harmless as "I'm just off to the shops/garage/pub", when in fact it's a restful few hours that only you enjoy. The key is to get a regular visit established – after all a garden doesn't look after itself, the weeds will take over, it all requires watering, etc etc.

Mother Teresa potatoes

If you're the scientific type, you could have a go at solving a problem that has so far beaten the rest of us. You'll have seen photos of misshapen and twisted root vegetables, caused (the experts say) by stones and other obstructions in the soil. Once in a while a really good one emerges and finds its way into the newspapers – a potato that resembles Mother Teresa, for example.

This suggests that in principle it should be possible to deliberately grow potatoes into particular shapes. Yet I can report that experiments with clay moulds don't work – the little potato, despite remaining connected to the main plant, just withers and dies in the airless chamber.

You can see where this is going. Why not start thinking about other options – perhaps a fibreglass mould with plenty of holes to let in air, and some light?

There could be big money in this. Just imagine the day when your website allows people to upload a photo of themselves, or better still their family and friends, and 6 months later they receive a bag of potatoes each in the shape of that person's head. What a great birthday gift!

And we haven't even started on carrots. This research and testing could make your gardening a truly exciting adventure.

What if you already have a garden?

Ok, this does make it tougher to get an allotment as well. You could try:

- Paying for a gardener to look after the home garden, while you go off to the allotment. Tricky, but worth a try - especially if you can find a handsome chap.

- Getting your wife or children to look after it.

- Having just a lawn at home, 'for the kids', making it unsuitable for vegetables.

- Put in attractive-sounding trees and shrubs whose shade prevents you having a decent vegetable plot at home.

- Failing all else, move to a new home without a garden.

How to get an allotment

Your local Council will tell you how. Allotments have an interesting social history, most of them being developed after the first world war for returning soldiers to be able to grow food for their families during tough economic times (at moments of domestic strife about your hobby you may want to remind your wife of this, with a sentimental – and if necessary, invented – family story about your grandad's allotment and how much it meant to him).

A parting thought - on most allotments it is legal to keep chickens, bees, and even goats...

Let's (re-)start a band

Everyone is doing it. And in our fifties it has a wonderfully free and relaxing feel, compared to being in a band in one's youth. No more ambition for fame and riches, no more fierce arguments and resentments, criticising of each other's musical abilities, or jockeying for centre-stage - just some pals having a laugh and belting out sounds. Bliss.

If you played in a band as a young man, this is going to be surprisingly easy. (And you probably did – leastways just about everyone in my home town was either in a band, in-between bands, or starting their own. Can so much dreadful home-grown music have ever been made in any one generation as during the 1970s?) Once you have played an instrument you never really forget how to, and the equipment nowadays is massively improved, and easier to carry.

The kit

If you remember heavy, expensive amplifiers with separate, huge, expensive loudspeaker cabinets (4 x 12 inch being the desired minimum speaker arrangement, and the stronger the magnet on each speaker, the better), all with unreliable and sometimes dangerous electrics, you are in for a treat. The amp and speaker combos of today are a joy – light, tiny, reliable and hugely powerful. How did they do that? While our backs were turned, it seems, the development of musical instruments and their amplification has never ceased to evolve, in the same way that typewriters evolved into laptops, tin cans and string into smartphones, and all the rest of it.

If you were in a teenage band you probably remember how badly you wanted a PA system but couldn't afford it (and didn't have space for all those stacks of loudspeakers). So instead you had to plug the microphones into the guitar amplifiers, creating horribly muddy, muffled singing. Well now a PA system is suddenly affordable, high quality, and tiny – you can pretty much fit one into the pockets of a tweed jacket. Incredible what progress they've made!

Choice of music and instrument

Not as easy as it may seem. If you had a rock band as a young man, you'll just do that again, right? And if possible with your old band members. But think carefully – is rock what you want, in your fifties? Can you really carry it off, all that posing and strutting, trying to look cool? People may laugh at you. It might be worth considering something a bit less heroic, less active, more suited to one's time of life. Skiffle, for example. Or even country rock, that you used to look down on with such disdain. Either it's changed or you have, because it doesn't sound half bad these days. And you can sit down to play.

Never played an instrument?

Don't let this put you off. The advantage of choosing simpler musical styles like skiffle or country is that everyone can take part. Even if you didn't play in a band when you were younger, or never learned an instrument, you can pick up spoons, a washboard, penny whistle, mouth organ or even a ukulele and play it within minutes (well, hours) because thanks to the internet it's much easier to learn everything now. Even a banjo isn't all that tricky.

Failing all else you could take up the bass guitar, a simple to learn but for some reason deeply unpopular instrument. Possibly connected to the fact that it's difficult to show off – I mean, stand out – while playing one. Learning the basics of the bass means you'll have almost no competition and plenty of opportunities to play.

Music without a band

Even if you can't be bothered forming a band, thanks to the internet you can still record complex musical arrangements in your own home (or shed), so I'm told. You could even, god help us, make it available online for others to hear. Remember to call this a hobby. And, most of all, don't share with anyone your unrealistic dreams of turning it into a new career.

Getting a lads' holiday

To some readers a lad's holiday may be nothing special – you already go on one each year, with your wife happily waving you off (not too happily, one hopes). To other readers, a lads' holiday may seem an unlikely dream. If that's you, here are some pointers to getting what you want.

First get some lads, by which I mean men of around your age who are friends from school, university, work, the pub, etc. You may need to identify a sub-group of three or four who can get along well enough for a few days in each other's company.

This group could well be the same one that you meet regularly in the pub, if you've managed to do that (see the earlier chapter on Pubs).

Find some kind of shared interest activity holiday on which to base a short break away from wives and family. A suitable activity could be sport (cycling), hunter-gatherer (fishing), pub-based (darts, the study of pub architecture), or what you will.

Crucially, don't make it sound too interesting. Archaeology or steam engines are ideal, putting off 99%

of wives. If you can't agree on one activity, settle for a walking holiday. Remember, think dull!

It's vital to choose a dismal-sounding destination, preferably one where it rains a lot. A British person has lots of options here. Ditto a Canadian. If you're based in the US, I guess you have Oregon. If Australia, perhaps somewhere crocodile-infested with plenty of bush fires.

Next, you need to get domestic approval.

Why you need to get away

It's quite unpredictable how your other half will respond to this idea. You may get lucky. This is most probably because she is looking for some equally large domestic favour. It could be a women-only holiday, a painfully expensive family trip, or evenings in insanely costly restaurants where you will feel out of place and looked down on by everyone, especially the waiters, and get robbed blind while having to dress up and pretend that everything is sublime and exquisite, even as you crave a pie and pint.

However it's in your interests to simply run with your luck and take, or try to dodge, your punishments later.

But if you meet resistance, of the firm sort or the complaining sort, here are your key phrases:

- "It's only for a few days."
- "We haven't done this sort of thing for 30 years."
- "It'll be a nice break for you, too."

- "You keep telling me I need exercise, well here it is."
- "I hardly ever see [Name] any more" – this being a friend your wife approves of, if there is one. (It doesn't matter if he's actually going on the trip or not, you can say later he dropped out.)

Remember that a tug at the heartstrings is always worth a try, if you can strike the appropriate note of manly, stoical wistfulness:

- "It's mainly for old Fred, he's not been too well / lost his allotment / lost his job / got divorced."
- "My dad / granddad / uncle always went away with his pals for a few days" (take out handkerchief)
- "I doubt we'll have a chance to do this again" (you will, of course - twice a year from now on)
- "I don't want to tell the boys I can't go, do I?"

Interestingly you will probably find it easier to get away for a lads holiday now you are in your fifties than you would have 20 years ago. Your wife will dismiss the idea that you are thinking about mischief with other women. And she is probably right, damn it.

Make it regular

Even if the holiday is only ok rather than wonderful, make sure you book up another one next year:

- "Well, I promised I'd go again."
- "I can't back out now, they'll think I don't like them or something."
- "Fred already booked the trip."

The crucial success is to establish a firm beachhead on the social landscape, snatching a good chunk of your time for yourself, every year. It's surprising how satisfying this feels. My guess is that we are tapping into something deep in our genetic history, when men went on the hunt for days on end, and no doubt also drank too much fermented tree bark and tried to get off with the women of other tribes, as well as hunting for wildebeest or whatever.

The other half [9]

Probably the only benefit to getting on in years is the accumulation of knowledge – perhaps 'wisdom' is a bit of a stretch. We have learned the hard way.

What women don't want

If there's something older geezers know, it's the things that profoundly annoy and madden our other halves:

Crankish behaviour

For example, while out walking with your partner it's unwise to shout "fall off!" at a passing youth on a skateboard. To us this seems an entirely reasonable reaction to an idiotic wheeled activity that should have died out years ago[10], but your partner for some reason takes it as evidence that you're becoming a crank and curmudgeon.

---

[9] Not a chapter about beer, sorry

[10] with the added benefit that they very likely will fall off, as happens all the time in this pointless 'sport'

Similarly, let's say you are out walking with your wife on a cloudy day, and you spot a young man ostentatiously wearing sunglasses. Your loud comment to the effect that blind people really shouldn't come out without their dog, rather than being appreciated as an apt bon-mot to puncture pretension, will be received by her with embarrassment and irritation. And ditto if you mutter 'Beaver' at a passing beard-owning hipster.

No matter how tempting, you just can't behave normally when out with your other half, and nor can you right wrongs, or poke fun at halfwits.

Being bored

Instead you have to entertain her with interesting and amusing stories and gossip, and not something she's heard fifty times already, either. Of course this is exceptionally difficult for most men, and hardly fair of her, either – she should expect such entertainment only from her female friends and relatives. It's our job to dispose of rotting vegetables from the back of the fridge, or sort out the problem when a light bulb needs changing, not to keep her entertained.

Excessive displays of affection

Women don't want some kind of simpering fool for a husband, who invents little endearing names for his beloved, showers her with gifts, praises her looks and style, cooks her special meals, and generally behaves like a love-struck nitwit. If you tend towards this kind of behaviour, even if only occasionally, you can expect to find your partner becoming increasingly exasperated, and irritated, telling you to 'man up' and wishing, possibly out loud, that you could be more of the strong, silent type.

The solution? Try acting cool and indifferent, pretend to be deep in manly thought, go off for long walks on your own, forget her birthday, refrain from displays of public affection; and before long you will be referring to the next section for advice.

Lack of affection

If you tend more towards the strong, silent type, expect to receive increasing levels of complaint from your wife that you are not affectionate enough, don't care about her, are too remote and disengaged, never show your feelings or even give her a hug, must be secretly seeing someone else, and so forth. Expect sulking, tears and long phone calls to sisters and friends (during which your instinct is no doubt either to turn the TV up louder, or go down the pub).

The remedy is clear: show some affection, buy some flowers, give her a pet name, hug her in public, surprise her with non-birthday gifts, and praise her looks and style. Before long you will need to refer to the previous section for advice.

What we need

UK readers may remember the Innovations catalogue – a small but fascinating booklet that arrived with the Sunday newspapers at random intervals. The whole thing was devoted to gadgets, and clearly aimed at men, with our natural interest in tools, hardware and electronic wizardry.

Some of the innovative gadgets could just about be useful in a pinch, while others were bizarre, pointless, but somehow still tempting.

Sadly the Innovations catalogue seems to have ceased publication. But it's high time we had a new catalogue appealing to the fifties age group, packed with clever-but-sensible gadgetry to solve our particular problems.

So if you're a millionaire with time on your hands, please get in touch. Until then, have a look at the proposals on the following pages – a few suggestions for useful items, provided by an innovative and technically-minded pub-based focus group.

Indoor scratching post

Indoor scratching post

For men, 'itchy-back syndrome' is a daily irritant. This robust yet elegant coir-matting scratching post is the solution (doubles as a punch ball).

Guinness gloves

Guinness gloves

Guinness nowadays is served at a brutally cold temperature, in the hope that young people will mistake it for lager. Bring it to a drinkable state with these unique heat-radiating gloves.

Adventure slippers

Adventure slippers

Go anywhere, full-comfort footwear. Ideal for muddy allotments, a quick game of football in the garden, or just taking a well-earned rest.

'Quiet please' signs

'Quiet please' signs

Carry a dozen folded in your pocket.
When you arrive at the pub, put them
on the tables around you (preferably
before other people arrive) and
marvel at the effect. Also useful in
cafes and restaurants, and on trains.

Mini blowtorch for ear and nose hair

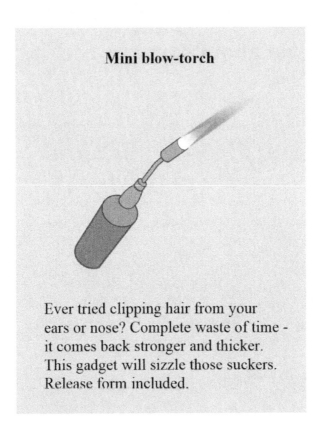

Mini blow-torch

Ever tried clipping hair from your
ears or nose? Complete waste of time -
it comes back stronger and thicker.
This gadget will sizzle those suckers.
Release form included.

What about skydiving?

Ah yes, the dangerous sports - hang-gliding, bungee jumping, potholing, wild water kayaking, and the rest. I hope this book has persuaded you of the interest, enjoyment, companionship and fun to be had from simpler pursuits. There is really no need to get all dressed up in gaudy outfits and put on a helmet that makes you look like an idiot rather than a mountaineer, to go bouncing off cliffs or delving into caves. You will almost certainly end up doing yourself a nasty injury and needing help from young people, who will smile patronisingly as they winch you into the air ambulance.

Dressing up and pursuing extreme sports shouts "Look how young I am!" even more loudly and unconvincingly than tattooing it on your forehead. Leave such foolishness to the young – they deserve it!

The End

Other books by PK Munroe

'**How Not to be a Tourist in London**' is packed with unusual advice for visitors to the capital. Essential reading for the unwary traveller!

'**You Can Stick It**' contains over 300 full-colour peelable stickers designed to assist the British public and the authorities. The book was published in December 2010 by The Friday Project, a division of Harper Collins.

An e-book of 'You Can Stick It' is available from online retailers, including iBooks and Amazon. The stickers are not peelable, however.

'**The Pub Letters**' is an e-book of inventions, schemes and proposals to improve public life, suggested to well-known companies and individuals, including the Pope and the British Royal Family. Originally published as 'The Thursday Night Letters' (New Holland Publishers, 2007) this book consists of the letters sent and the replies received.

Connect with the author online

A blog showcasing his activities:

http://youcanstickit.blogspot.co.uk

Printed in Great Britain
by Amazon